ROCK SOLID

IN

ALL SEASONS

THE BUSINESSPERSON'S DASHBOARD

Do not ignore the warning signals

DAVID MUGUN

Rock Solid in All Seasons

© David Mugun, 2017

All rights reserved. No part of this publication may be reproduced, stored in a retrieval system or transmitted in any form or by any means, electronic, mechanical, photocopying, recording or otherwise without the prior written permission of the copyright owner.

Published by the Scribe Centre

Nairobi, Kenya

Table of Contents

ACKNOWLEDGEMENT 5

INTRODUCTION 6

THE PURPOSE OF BUSINESS. 7

1. Not attracting business risk. 10

2. Not retaining business risk. 13

3. Political risk. 15

4. Lack of cash risk 17

5. Business systems risk 20

6. Reputational risk 39

7. Euphoria Risk. 41

8. Resources risk. 51

9. The arrival pitfall risk. 53

10. Latent disdain risk 55

11. Technological risk. 59

12. Business environment awareness risk. 62

CASE STUDY -THE THREE "WISE" MEN OF APPLE COUNTY. 63

DEDICATION

To the businessperson who wants to run a rock solid business.

ACKNOWLEDGEMENT

To Almighty God, for enabling me to complete my third book.

To my family for the constant encouragement.

To all those that participated in the training sessions whose content resulted in this book.

INTRODUCTION

This book owes its inspiration to the planning notes that were used to develop, a two-hour training session for owners of small and medium-sized businesses.

The sessions in different locations had positive reviews from most participants for a number of reasons.

First, they wanted it kept simple and free of ambiguity.

Second, they loved it delivered with short topics so that the two hours were value for time.

Participants also wanted a practical chance to discuss all the business risks mentioned, in the program. This was achieved through a case study session in small groups. This forms the last chapter.

In all, twelve business risks are covered. Enjoy reading the book.

THE PURPOSE OF BUSINESS.

The question "why are we in business?" normally generates a myriad of answers. The most common are:-

To make profit

To use our talents.

To pass time.

To work, because we inherited a business or some wealth from our parents.

To give back to society.

The reality is that we are in business to attract and retain customers. Again, we are in business, **to attract and retain customers.** Our efforts, behaviors, and plans must at all times revolve around attracting and retaining. When we operate outside of the core reasons for being in business, we tread into risky territory.

The activities around attracting and retention of business, sum up to create growth.

Continuous growth ensures that our path to profitability is assured.

Businesses experience growth and stagnant phases also known as business cycles. These, in turn, affect how we attract or retain customers. Sometimes it is prudent to shift our efforts towards retaining customers and at other times, circumstances dictate that we attract more customers aggressively.

Whenever big decisions such as an impending national budget are on the way, a general election or plebiscite, business people tend to slow down their decision making because such events have an impact on business.

Far too many businesses also experience slowdowns in times of recession, or, even as a result of industry specific raw materials shortages. Reasons abound.

So, attracting and retaining customers are the constants but several variables may undermine our good intentions.

We shall focus on twelve risks that can undermine business. As we focus on the twelve risks, let us bear in mind the following observations.

"Choices have consequences and they have a cost."

"Everything as we know it is the way it is, because of the actions that were taken or the lack of them."

"A brand is the positive emotional connection associated with a product or service, an individual or organization. It will normally include product quality, character and other tangible and intangible attributes."

1. Not attracting business risk.

When we cannot attract business, our expenses end up consuming the little money that exists. There are known reasons why business is not coming our way.

First, our selling skills are not up to speed. Customers tend to appreciate your competition better than you.

Our selling skills must go beyond the expected product knowledge that requires us to know the features, advantages, and benefits of what we sell.

The sale begins long before we plan to get into a business. How people view us or know of us is critical to our success.

If a doctor is reputed as a philanderer, patients will avoid him for fear of falling victim. Even if that were the best doctor in his area of specialization, his variables will have outdone his core business or constants.

A very able consultant by day and an apparent drunkard by night will not inspire confidence in potential and existing clients.

Established reputations often precede us. Everything that we do shapes up the outcome of our selling and it is, therefore, important to maintain enviable reputations.

2. When customers have the benefit of a higher experience than your offering, they tend to perceive your product as inferior even if they had been buying it before.

Take the case of your hitherto favorite restaurant. Perhaps you like it because of its proximity to your office or, very much so because of the orderliness and quality of food and service.

At one point in time, you happen to be in another restaurant. This particular one has newer décor, fancy cutlery and everything in it exceeds your expectations. You immediately fall in love with it and update your criteria of a good restaurant.

When you return to your previously wonderful eatery, you will immediately feel that the standards have gone down even if, nothing has changed.

This feeling is triggered by your higher experience. In the same way, if we maintain our standards in isolation of the realities around us, customers will desert us for higher experiences.

It pays to look around. Do some competitor analysis.

3. We must also deliver what we promise. Recently, I witnessed a disturbing event. A friend and I pulled over to a little farmers market to buy farm fresh fruits as we journeyed upcountry.

As we awaited our attendant to return with our change money from the purchase, a Matatu pulled over and a vendor rushed to display his decent fish catch to interested passengers.

One person chose a large sized fish and paid for it. The vendor then suspended it by the Matatu's wipers as is the tradition.

When the customer turned away to return to his seat, the vendor replaced the procured fish with a smaller one. The owner could only know of it once he had reached his destination.

If we do not deliver our promise at all times, then we run the risk of desertion.

2. Not retaining business risk.

There are people who are very good at attracting business because of wonderful selling skills. The same may not be said of them when retention is required. Some plausible reasons include:-

The presence of very poor customer service skills.

Customers seldom appreciate handlers who show no concern for them or empathize with their needs.

Sometimes, familiarity breeds contempt and we begin to take our customers for granted because, they have returned to us so many times, that we now think that they will do so till kingdom come.

Customers are human, and they can read and tell how we value them, based on how we handle them. They will make the decision to keep supporting us or not, based on our own actions.

We may have the wrong people handling our customers because their personality type comes out too aggressively or too snobbish for the liking of customers.

If we cannot keep appreciating them or acknowledging them every time that they support our businesses, then we set up ourselves for desertion.

The worst thing to do with clients is to be seen to be experimenting on them. They must feel fairly treated.

3. Political risk.

Political risk is one threat that not only undermines our business attraction and retention endeavors but, can also create actual losses curtsey of overcharged emotions.

Politicians are inspiring and, or repulsive in equal measure depending on whose side you are.

When decisions are made emotionally rather than rationally, it interferes with the same emotional space that our hard earned brand occupies. The last thing that we talked about in chapter 1 was branding and you may wish to refer again.

The same favorable emotional appeal that brings customers to us can turn them away if our political preferences oppose rather than complement each other.

As a precaution, take it that your customer base will invariably have supporters of all the political players in question and will embrace those that align and reject anyone of a contrary opinion to their own.

As a business person, it is, therefore, important to remain highly conscious of political events and discussions that can undermine our continuous duty of attracting and retaining business.

It is prudent to take up insurance cover against political events whilst coming out as a neutral observer so that your business emotional appeal remains intact.

4. Lack of cash risk

The famous saying "cash is king" sums it up. When we run out of money, we become desperate.

Desperate times call for drastic measures. Anything out of desperation has the potential to leave you worse than you were before.

It is imperative on the business person to ensure that all sources of cash do not run dry. The first of cause is to guard our emotional appeal to our target market so that we continuously attract and retain business.

The risks discussed so far and those in the succeeding chapters, work, in combination to ensure that money keeps flowing or gets cut out depending on how you navigate them.

The second source is your immediate supporters such as family members or investors. Doubts of you by this group are your doom and gloom.

The rule here is, always work in a way that they keep asking you for opportunities to invest because they see value.

When people want to invest in your business, it is an assurance that when the real need for cash comes, you have it ready.

The third source is the bank and like your second group above, the bank is the greatest adherer of the saying that "money follows orderliness."

If all the business fundamentals are sound, the bank will always step in to support when needed. The relationship with the bank always calls for a proactive approach and never a reactive one.

If we work such that we are always ready for a loan facility, then the bank will always be willing.

Unfortunately, too many business people let things go out of hand and then, plead with the bank for support.

No doubt, keeping all the fundamentals intact is a difficult task. The next chapter shall cover business systems risk and will shade more light on how to remain organized.

When our relationship with the bank is intact, we face the temptation of testing our relationship with the bank and may end up borrowing what we never needed or planned for.

We must always spend borrowed money on what it is intended for.

Credit is best left to the banks. If we must, we should only do so to tried and tested customers. The best credit seekers usually have the best stories and their tomorrow hardly comes. This leaves you in trouble.

It is prudent to have a credit policy that is in writing and also requires a credit seeker to fill in a form that will then justify or help you to decline the request.

The form must also have a sign-up section for the debtor to confirm that he owes you money and that it is due by a certain date.

When people sign for credit, they are taking responsibility and are more likely to pay up. When they do not pay, you have with you a signed up agreement that you can use in court to recover your money.

5. Business systems risk.

Systems keep us organized. They help us to capture all transactions and help us keep the useful history of all important things to us.

A good business mind has its limits besides, the brain is fallible. We forget or we get caught up in other important matters outside of business.

We know that honesty adds to our emotional appeal with customers and other stakeholders in our business. Systems help us to remain true to our own businesses as well as all interested parties.

A true account of the happenings in our business enables us to make useful reports and obtain precious feedback. Systems help to keep us proactive rather than reactionary.

We are then able to manage repeat cycles such as re-order levels, business permit and insurance renewals, association memberships and many others.

In nature, the human mind tends to avoid what is viewed as complex or difficult to attain.

Systems development and implementation are among those actions that are misconstrued as difficult yet, it is actually their absence that complicates our business dealings.

Good systems and processes, give us the peace of mind needed to stick to our core business, attracting and retaining customers. We have also seen earlier, that money follows orderliness.

We know of people who have several businesses and keep adding new ones. The common thread that runs through all that they do, is putting systems and processes in place.

Such people go beyond what most business people do with systems. They put in place structures that work even when they are not part of the business.

Many people develop processes that only work when they are part of the equation.

When one is urgently called to attend a meeting or to attend to a misfortune, they prefer to shut down their business or not go out at all.

This fear is synonymous with bad or ineffective systems and processes.

We know of businesses run by people outside of this country and even the continent yet, they make good profits because they have sound management teams working for them. Well- run multinational organizations come into mind here.

Good systems give them the confidence to employ others to take care of business.

A good starting point is to document all processes and share them with all who need to know in your business.

It may take days. If you started your business without a consultant, then you do not require one to document your systems and processes. This can be done in-house.

You should only call for help if they need to be automated.

When everyone knows what is expected of them, they provide uniform service levels to all customers.

You will avoid situations where a customer prefers to return to your premises after lunch, just because their preferred employee in your business is out.

Let me use a simple business as an example of why systems are important.

An enterprising business person decides to have something to do on the side, to augment his salary.

He chooses to run a meat outlet that is fashioned on the typical tree stump, meat hooks, machete and an axe setup that we have all come to know.

He hires an experienced attendant taken from a competing outlet and lets him run the business.

Every day, the owner checks on his starting meat stock by weighing the cow, goat and sheep carcasses. He also counts the cash in the till then sets off to work.

His meat is the best in town because it is sourced from a farm that is known for good animal husbandry.

Everyone that he meets on his daily visit to the outlet thinks that business is brisk. This is on account of the number of customers streaming in throughout the day.

The day-end review shows that the meat left in stock, and the cash in the till, add up and nothing is missing. The only puzzle is that of too many customers buying but the stock never runs out.

One weekend, the owner decided to attend to his meat business and worked the whole day in the outlet. He discovered that the meat ran out by mid-morning and again by late afternoon.

He also discovered that his preferred supplier was the same one that replenished his business meat stock on a daily basis.

The regular attendant was at pains to explain where the extra sales went to. It is obvious that the business person was conned on a daily basis.

This is just one outlet. We are told of a famous politician in Nairobi who was the biggest in the meat business and had several outlets before his death.

This famous meat business giant, armed with little formal education never lost a kilogram of meat in any of his outlets yet, he hardly frequented any of them. We shall come back to this successful business person.

So how did our enterprising businessman get it wrong?

In order to get answers, let us study what he did right, then, the wrong things that got him cleaned out.

He got the business location right because it was easily accessible to most customers.

He got the supplier right because his preferred source was known for quality practices that led to quality meat.

On the wrong side of things, he employed an experienced attendant so that things could move on smoothly.

The only problem here was that the attendant knew the dark secrets of the trade and found a clueless newcomer to exploit.

The saying "if you do not inspect, then do not expect" is true on two fronts in this case.

First, the business person was too eager to get started and never did his due diligence on the employee.

Second, he never cared to agree with the supplier on supply cycles. This is obvious because of his inexperience.

The attendant ended up pocketing most of the daily sales income for a long time because the owner never gave the business the correct level of attention.

So what did the famous meat business giant that we read of earlier do to get things right?

First, he got his locations and sources of meat right. He had the correct level of experience because he had started off with a single outlet.

Armed with requisite experience, he tied all the loose ends and agreed with the supplier to have all deliveries documented and reconciled daily and also at end-month.

He also put in place rules so that the outlets had to reorder for more meat once a certain stock level was breached.

Our meat business giant, also never let a chance pass him when an opportunity to make a memorable example of a bad employee, presented itself.

He made enough noise of it so that no other person in the business could hire anyone he fired for stealing from him.

He also took his business audits seriously and followed through the outcome seriously.

Finally, whenever he had a new employee, he personally spent time in the specific outlet for as long as it took to get the new staff member settled down at work.

This is a simple business example and we have hardly exhausted everything that was needed to get things right. The little that we have shared helps us appreciate the need for a culture of systems and processes.

The same example dispels the myth that one must be physically present in the business throughout to avoid incidences of pilferage and wanton theft.

In reality, what must be present throughout are proper systems and processes.

Business systems risk, also covers having systems in place that can be breached. When this happens, it compromises system integrity.

We have heard of people capable of hacking into computer systems to steal customer information. In some instances, banking systems have been broken into and customers have lost money.

So if big institutions are vulnerable, then small businesses are at an obvious risk.

It is prudent, to have an information technology expert at your beck and call so that your business systems are constantly checked for any inherent and new risks.

Systems and processes on their own are not useful if the essential management skills are missing. How we handle everything is very important.

The following six soft skills are of paramount importance.

Delegation, Coaching, Emotional intelligence, Supervising others, Performance management, and Negotiation skills.

Delegation is often executed in a manner that results in the abdication of business. No guidance is given to whoever is taking up the assigned tasks.

When delegating a task, it is important to clearly think through what it is you intend to have someone else do in your place.

Write down the objectives and the results that you expect. Clearly determine how long the task will run and, put in place clear timelines for reviewing, and for ending of the assignment.

Have a meeting with your designated person and explain your mission to them.

If the task is a continuous one, then consider making it part of the person's job description.

The delegation of tasks or duties has a clear beginning and an end.

Coaching is a key skill that the business person must have. There is always a moment that requires coaching to take place.

Coaching in itself is the process through which an experienced person passes knowledge and skills to a less experienced person, in a way that the less experienced one, is encouraged to bring out options to reaching a solution.

In comparison, training would have the more experienced person passing down all the knowledge and skills.

So, when coaching those looking up to you for leadership, it is critical that you create an atmosphere of tolerance to ideas from them.

It is possible to have coaching running throughout your relationship with the staff member or person in question.

Many times, the lessons stick better when the learner is involved in the process, and this is a skill that businesspeople are encouraged to use, as often as possible.

Emotional intelligence is the ability to recognize understand and manage our own emotions whilst recognizing understanding and influencing those of others.

The importance of emotional intelligence comes out best when one is under pressure. Take the case of someone in the crockery business.

A customer has walked in to buy a set of six tumblers, from a shop reputed for fast service. The shop attendant is eager to impress his boss and rushes to the shop storeroom to bring the wanted set.

As he approaches the counter at a fast pace, he trips over and three tumblers get broken into hundreds of pieces in the process.

Let us take a slow motion analysis of what is exactly happening.

First, the customer needs a quick solution to the set of tumblers and will feel duped if the service levels do not match up to the reputation of the shop.

Second, the attendant knows that he has created a loss by damaging the three tumblers and must face his boss and the customer at the same time.

He must still be part of the solution even when he has caused a problem albeit accidentally.

The boss understands the extent of his loss in the glasses and also knows that the customer can walk away thus, compounding the loss through a missed opportunity.

Now, back to real time, the shop owner has two scenarios to choose from.

The first is to react by insulting the attendant and reading out the riot act. He may act in total disregard of the customers present and loudly moan his loss.

Second, he may ask the attendant to go back and fetch another set from the store room, and have the customer happy first, then deal with the loss later.

Both scenarios are options available under pressure.

If the boss opts for the second setting, then he will have cleverly recognized, understood and managed his own emotions whilst recognizing, understanding and influencing those of the customer and attendant.

Remember that at the beginning, we said that our efforts, behaviours, and plans must at all times revolve around attracting and retaining customers. In so doing, we remain in business.

Supervising others is a critical skill. The example of the shop owner above provides us with a perfect example of when both, coaching and supervisory skills are needed the most.

One of the rules of supervision is to praise good performance in the open and reprimand in private.

As the business grows, the need for more people becomes apparent. Even at the initial stages, a business will require the services of delivery people or service providers of all kinds.

Even if these people may not be our employees, they need our supervision just as much as our own do, so that no process of our core business of attracting and retaining customers is compromised.

Supervision combines managerial and leadership skills and knowledge to get things done.

Management is about the control of resources such as financial, human, tools and all the things that a business needs.

In management, none conformity attracts consequences.

Leadership is about inspiring people to achieve desired objectives.

Both management and leadership are required when supervising people.

Management should principally revolve around the systems, processes, and strategies that we have put in place so that we are seen to be fair to our customers, staff and shareholders.

Leadership will largely focus on the big picture of the overall success of the business.

In supervising others, boundaries must be set beforehand. People want to enjoy what they do or at least, have a bearable work environment.

An atmosphere of professionalism is required when supervising others. It is not a license to bully. It is a responsibility that one must keep in mind that the end goal, is to contribute to the process of attracting and retaining customers.

Performance management is a process and not an event. It is an impartial process void of favoritism.

In order to succeed in performance management, one must set all the expected objectives in advance. Normally we have New Year objectives set before the year ends.

It is one of the most important functions of the business and must be given the level of attention and seriousness that it deserves.

This is one thing that must be embedded in the systems and processes of the business.

It is critical to understand the things that our business requires us to pay attention to in coming up with what to manage.

Going back to the meat outlet story, the successful owner put in place restocking levels such that more meat could be delivered before the one on display ran out.

In reviewing performance after persistent stockouts, the meat outlet owner would seek to understand if the problem was internal or external.

Internal would mean that the restocking policy is not adhered to and in which case, he would know where to turn his performance management attention to.

External would mean that the supplier is either too slow or, not having enough meat to deliver. The business owner would then turn his attention to the correct people.

Someone must be responsible for performance management and must bring up any observable gaps in performance for attention.

The overall performance of the business must contribute to enabling the business to better attract and retain customers.

Negotiation is the process that precedes the giving or taking of value. One party gives value while the other gains value in exchange for money or any acceptable alternative.

The most important thing about negotiation is how the process concludes. An ideal situation is a win-win position where both parties are happy with the outcome.

There are people who never get to negotiate a second time with the same person because they believe in winning at the expense of the other party. This is always short lived because word gets around quickly about bad negotiators.

It is prudent to keep the details of negotiations away from those not involved, even long after the process.

People, who boast of how they got a good deal by portraying the other party in a bad light, are to be avoided because the next time, it is your story that will be told to others.

The negotiation process is always part of business, and the better you are at it, the more likely that you will keep control of your core objectives, of attracting and retaining customers.

A good bargain with your suppliers is a win for your clients because they will buy at a better price when you pass down the gains of a better negotiation.

Emotional intelligence plays a key role in any negotiation. It is a skill that can be coached and also delegated. This shows how the other skills are intertwined.

6. Reputational risk.

Nothing follows a man more than his shadow. Reputation does the same. Everything that we have covered so far has a bearing on reputation.

How we negotiate, supervise others or manage performance impacts the impression of us to others.

The best intentions of a man with a bad reputation are never taken seriously.

A good medical doctor is someone that society respects because he keeps the secrets of many patients. The same doctor can become a pariah if he breaks that trust.

The best management consultant in town is one to seek guidance from. The same person, if seen indulging in excesses such as alcohol abuse and promiscuous endeavors, will lose his shine and appeal to would-be clients.

The combined eye of the public is too big to hide from, and its ubiquity can never be fooled forever.

Negative news spreads faster than positive news. The reputation of the business, its owner and employees influence purchasing decisions.

People with good reputations can overcome malicious acts of bad competitors because everyone knows them to be steadfast in their dealings.

A bad or doubtful reputation can turn the bank away when you need it most. Here, how we guard our systems is crucial.

Our standards must be adhered to and managed well so that we are consistent in service delivery.

A bad reputation undermines our ability to attract and retain customers. If you have reached such a state, save your business by taking a back seat and allow a trusted person to lead the business.

It pays to be the person that everyone admires.

7. Euphoria Risk.

Euphoria is defined as a state of intense happiness and self-confidence or seen another way, euphoria is extreme happiness, sometimes more than is reasonable in a particular situation.

This state can flood anyone at any time in their business life. When a promise of good life, however, short lived; finds its way into someone's mind, the results can be mind-boggling.

Take the case of a life-changing multi-million business deal, that is now concluded but pending the final signature. The mind of a novice can turn euphoric and trigger several financial commitments with no supporting money.

The deal is not yet done until the final signature is appended and the initial deposit received. Should the deal abort, then the businessman is sunk and the business is destroyed.

A good business streak can also heighten euphoria risk. When good amounts of money come in unexpectedly, we may get tempted to expand the business too quickly or channel the funds elsewhere without checking if the business actually needed it.

A politician can ask for your support on the campaign trail in exchange for business once in office.

It is a gamble that can go either way and can drain both financial resources and the much needed entrepreneurial energy that the business needs.

To overcome euphoria, we need to consider the following.

First, we need an accountability partner. This is someone from outside your business who is trustworthy and can tell you things that can aid your business.

An accountability partner can bring in objectivity, and many times will tell you what you don't want to hear, but knows that it is good for the business.

They can be volunteers or on an agreed stipend.

If the business can afford it, upgrade the accountability partners into a board of advisors or directors.

Advisors, unlike directors, have no legal duties to the business. Directors have a legal duty and with the help of your lawyer, you can craft a good agreement to manage the relationship.

When you take the accountability partner route, pick someone or people who can complement your strengths.

It is also important to appreciate that your selection process must be done carefully to avoid exposing yourself to people with ill intentions.

A good starting point is to write down your strengths and weaknesses both personal and as a business.

Now build a profile of the kind of people who potentially can complement your strengths and weaknesses. Consider the following points.

Your candidates must be in a position to put in the time for meetings. There is no point of having a genius who is unavailable. Equally, it makes no sense to have a fool who is available to you.

Find people who have a track record and have other people who can vouch for their good standing.

Their contacts should count in your business so that it makes it easier to either transact business or overcome the myriad of challenges that afflict the business from time to time.

Go for expertise in areas crucial to the business. For instance, a good business development owner should look for a good financial brain, if that is his area of weakness.

Bring in useful experience to the business through seasoned people. Some people have plenty of experience that is not of any use to your business.

By all means, avoid trophy collectors. These are people whose egos are at ease when they serve on so many boards.

Watch out for reputational risk in your candidates.

Once you have your list of potential accountability partners, take your time to make your final picks. Approach them individually and tell them what is expected of them. Allow them to give you their expectations too.

When you have your accountability partner(s) in place, together, develop a calendar of meetings and articulate the objective of the meetings. Agree on the frequency of meetings. Will they be monthly or quarterly?

Also, agree on how to call for urgent meetings that have been necessitated by acts or issues crucial to the business.

Ensure that the minutes are written out and not left as mental notes because you are now part of an accountability process. If you can, have a dedicated minute taker.

The hardest thing about adapting the accountability partner route is the admission of past business sins to someone else. You may have tax issues or had dubious business practices.

The faster you confess them, the faster you get back on track. Entrepreneurship teething problems may cause you to focus on the urgent things and not the important things.

This will often get you into trouble or in a labyrinth of things that will later need urgent action. Overcome your fear and expose your sins, after all, you are getting into a time of accountability.

The second point on how to manage the euphoria risk is found in the all-time advice. In anything that you do, please do it in moderation.

The synonyms of the word moderation include – restraint, self-control, and balance. When you eat, do it in moderation. When you entertain or you are the one getting entertained, do it with self-control.

Anything excessive is wasteful and drains away much-needed resources. Anything that takes too much time, money and energy or any one of the three, must be re-examined and managed if it does not add anything to your core business or wellbeing.

A life of excesses eventually catches up when one is no good to himself or his business.

A famous man in this country now retired from politics and is nearing a hundred years of age, some time ago retired from the chairmanship of the board of a respected financial institution.

On the day of his farewell party, he was observed by the youthful employees, engaging in a conversation with his driver at the parking lot.

As the conversation went on, this old man, calmly raised one foot off the ground, and gently scratched an itching ankle without losing his balance.

A group of curious managers watching the goings-on soon gathered around, and asked the retiring chairman about his secret, given that many of his age mates had passed on.

With a grin, his answer was simple and powerful.

"In life, make sure that in everything that you do, do it in moderation."

The same man, for many years, has been known to enjoy his daily swim and gym workout.

Over the years, our good old man, a known stickler for rules and time has exercised plenty of self-control and has kept his sharp mind to his ripe age.

Our old man continues to enjoy life in moderation. We are no exception to this rule and must guard against excesses lest we get euphoric.

The third point on the containment of euphoria is the habit of thorough research on all the business dealings and plans.

Research helpfully slows us down into sobriety as we piece together our exciting thoughts.

Many entrepreneurs operate on gut feel as a consequence of experiences encountered, in their business dealings.

Over time, this becomes a habit that harbors deeply buried pitfalls that result in expensive lessons. Euphoria calls for instant attention, action, and energy and so does research.

Research takes many forms ranging from simple to complex approaches. This is largely dependent on the enormity of what is at hand.

Simple fact finding can save you your much-needed dime.

What if it was an idea deliberately thrown your way, by a competitor who is hell bent on destructing your attention on, what gives him the upper hand over golden opportunities?

More complex tasks that require research can be given to an expert or discussed with your accountability partner.

The fourth point on staving off euphoria is the application of the 80/20 rule or eighty, twenty rule named after the Italian economist Vilfredo Pareto

The rule states that, for many events, roughly 80% of the effects come from 20% of the causes. In business, it is a rule of thumb that 80% of your business comes from 20% of your clients.

Now putting this rule into practice all the time will make us ask ourselves if what we are working on is within the 20% of activities that generate 80% of our results.

Will your new idea positively add to the 20% of things that yield 80% of the results for you?

Euphoria is known to break all boundaries of reason known to man and, can make us engage in time-consuming activities that have no immediate value to us.

Many times, it will be at the expense of the tried and tested things, which keep us going.

I have observed on a number of occasions, that extremely successful people, never exhibit open excitement when they come across a good idea.

When they are at an event and someone brings out an idea with the potential to make tons of money, they make a mental note.

You will only know that they took note when you see the results of the execution.

The simple mind, when faced with the same good idea, will erupt loudly with euphoria. Always approach any new possibilities with a high sense of self-control.

8. Resources risk.

Businesses usually require being well resourced to thrive beyond the challenges in the market. Resources take the form of money, staff, property and tools.

We look at this risk from the fact that these resources can go missing by virtue of internal or external intervention.

Internal intervention relates to people inside the business. External intervention relates to people outside the business.

Internally, money and property can get stolen causing the business to suffer losses and stress from the lack of resources.

External forces can also conspire to mess the business. Fire from arsonists can cripple an enterprise or kill it all together. So how do we guard against these kinds of risks?

First, we must insure the business against all possible occurrences. Find suitable cover. Discuss the same with your insurance company or broker.

Second, we must have sound systems. This is intertwined with systems risk. Good systems will prevent or greatly minimize resource losses.

Third, as much as possible, avoid the use of or handling of cash. Work with electronic platforms like those for mobile money and credit cards where applicable. This minimizes the risks of being targeted by armed robbers and disloyal staff.

Have contracts that govern the relationship with your staff so that you are protected from all possibilities.

9. The arrival pitfall risk.

This is an interesting kind of risk and occurs when one thinks that he has arrived at the success destination permanently.

When ego and money cross paths to give one the sense of power over everybody, then the arrival pitfall has surely kicked in.

The presence of this risk is characterized by a change in speech, where one wants to dominate others because it is their opinion that matter above all others.

One is often surrounded by symbiotic sycophants. Ego stroking is rewarded with money, drinks and small gifts.

This is when success becomes a problem instead of a blessing.

Walking styles change and new status symbols become obvious.

This pitfall awakens reputational and euphoria risks and in combination, it is only a matter of time before the full meaning of "pride comes before a fall", actually comes into perspective.

This risk often times, comes from the actualization of deeply embedded desires that one was unable to fulfill before they made money.

It is also the result of bad or no mentorship. When you begin to fall, everyone can see it clearly except yourself. When the sycophants take off, then it is too late for you.

To overcome this risk or its possibility, it is paramount for us to have accountability partners who can help us navigate success.

No man is an island unto himself. Loop yourself around the experiences of other successful people and learn how to keep calm.

10. Latent disdain risk.

The word latent refers to something that exists but is inactive or hidden until it is awakened by the right conditions.

Disdain is the dislike for something or someone because they do not deserve your respect.

When used together, latent disdain refers to the hidden dislike for someone or thing and as a risk, it only comes to light when an alternative presents itself.

This is the risk that stays hidden in monopolistic businesses. Many other businesses also have this risk but it remains unknown to the business owner.

When you don't pay attention to your customers and you don't treat them well, the discomfort with your business builds up.

If customers come to you just because you are the only one of your type, then you must give them more reasons to come over.

There are monopolistic businesses that are very much liked by customers and the entry of competition does little to test their faith in the business.

Those that are liked deliberately resonate with customers' needs and wants and continuously research on what keeps them relevant.

Those that stock up hatred alongside merchandise on their shelves, just accumulate loads of latent disdain.

Take the case of a businessman suffering from the arrival pitfall and has plenty of pent-up latent disdain in his business.

The moment a competitor sets foot and opens shop, the opportunity to express disgust at the hitherto monopolistic business owner, is greeted with pomp and maybe even euphoria.

Unfortunately, many businesses have this risk and only get to know of it when it is too late. The only way out is to constantly review your offerings and their impact on customers. Customers tell you the truth all the time.

If anyone in your business is not providing excellent customer service, then they are killing your business. You must take action.

Whenever customers begin to sound like a bother, then change tack because they are the main reason for your existence as a business.

There is a famous building in town that affords its tenants an ideal location to do business. The owner has for several years thrived on the model that requires the payment of goodwill, the equivalent of a year's rent and then an additional six months' rent upfront.

This is after taking a similar amount in the rental deposit. For years, it has been his way or the highway to lesser locations.

Not too long ago, the building owner looked disturbed. He demanded answers from the caretaker, as to why the occupancy was steadily falling. The caretaker promised to respond once he had a plausible answer.

The caretaker started his investigation by reaching out to those, unsuccessful office space seekers who had left their contact details with him in the past.

A consistent pattern soon emerged. Not only were they uninterested in the building, they also did not wish to hear from the caretaker again.

Most of these would-be tenants had settled either in home offices or building hitherto viewed as less suitable.

The game changer was the fiber optic cabling that had been laid all over the city.

With WIFI connection, most people had the choice of utilizing Skype calls and other internet enabled advantages, to reach out and maintain their clientele.

The building remained empty for a long time until a university bought it out at a throwaway price.

The man finally caved into the latent disdain risk and, potential tenants put their money into better use than have to pay for goodwill, rent deposit and six months' rent upfront.

11. Technological risk.

The world today is positioned around technology. The story of the man and his building in the previous chapter captures what can happen when technology brings change.

The phone today is also a computer. You can transact business from your phone and save yourself the trouble of leaving your comfortable location to execute business.

It is possible to get punished by the market for lack of good technology.

It is also possible to suffer the misfortune of security breaches perpetrated by computer hackers who can steal useful information and use the same against you.

Banks have had their systems breached by hackers.

This risk has as many caution areas, as there are technology users but, some of the salient ones include the following.

Have a phone that can keep you linked to the world so that you have access to fresh information that you can then respond to on time.

Smartphones, do not have smart batteries. Please ensure that they are charged at all times. You could lose business for being offline.

Where possible, have your own home printer, computer, and scanner. Some of the most sensitive information is given away in bureaus.

I know of someone who was bidding for a big government project. He typed out the document at his office then saved it in a flash stick and had it printed at the bureau.

Because of the volume of work, some 1,000 pages, the work had to be saved into the bureau hard drive.

The document was well bound together and sealed in a fitting envelope, then, out the man went to drop it off at the tender box.

On reaching the box, he was informed of the postponement of the same by a week.

Meanwhile at the bureau, a friend of the competitor, went into print some work and came across the completed tender document. He quickly saved it into his flash stick and quietly handed over to his friend.

The competing friend used the new find to enrich his tender document and awaited the new deadline to drop off the bid.

It turned out, that the competitor aided by the bureau customer won the bid and proceeded to execute the assignment.

The loser forgot to delete the document once he was done and many weeks of work went down the drain. Just make sure that the same doesn't afflict you.

Ensure to safeguard all your passwords and frequently change them to avoid the same being known by the wrong people.

Finally, please have a technology expert on your side as mentioned in the earlier chapters.

12. Business environment awareness risk.

Most times, we only respond to what we know and never respond to what we don't know. In business, it can mean making or losing money.

If we keep ourselves out of useful information loops we kill or slow down our businesses.

It is important to get involved through business associations or a grouping near your area. We must network to know what is happening around us.

When networking, do it without giving away your advantage to competition. People go to networking forums with different agendas. Yours is to know what is new or going on around you.

Read continuously. Most successful business people the world over, attribute, part of their success to continuous reading. Do not be left out.

Now, please take the time to read the case study overleaf and use it to test your understanding of the 12 risks.

CASE STUDY - THE THREE "WISE" MEN OF APPLE COUNTY.

Apple County is home to entrepreneurs of all shades and businesses.

Here, everyone values peace just as much as, they value their respective businesses. Every five years, Apple county residents elect their leaders based on, who appeals to their needs or priorities the most.

Three investors of interest to us do business in Apple County.

Meet JJ, a successful hotelier. For the past four years, JJ's hotel, "The Apple hotel" has registered 60 % bed occupancy in the lowest days and, 100% occupancy for most of the month.

The Apple hotel is a favorite conferencing destination and, also a magnet for the moneyed locals and travelers at end month. Both the restaurant and the bar are beehives of activity.

The business meets its obligations to all its suppliers alongside, the bank for a business expansion loan taken three years ago.

As things look today, business is brisk and the bank has just approved a new facility for the planned expansion into phase two.

It is projected that in a year's time, the business must complete the new section lest it misses out on potential business.

There is an interesting observation. This year, the business is experiencing an abnormal boom time. It has become a must stop-over venue for many people.

Several people are coming over to discuss current affairs, and ordering for food and drinks in the process. With many people, money is flowing in.

The euphoria has caught on, and JJ has just been convinced by recently acquired revellers, to consider making an additional fortune, from his moneyed friends in the leadership race. "You can supply them with campaign material!" They shout.

To JJ, ideas coming from his customers, however, farfetched are welcome.

He always quips that "listening to customers is the key to success." And on that note, he throws them a new round of their favourite drink, in appreciation.

His preferred candidates for Senator, Lady county representative, and Governor have a team dubbed "team Inua Maisha" and together, they traverse the vast county campaigning at every stop for all on board.

The present leadership has never ever given JJ business and he is, therefore, eager for a change of guard.

Team Inua Maisha has promised JJ a minimum of twenty-four seminars per year, at The Apple hotel. Simple calculations indicate to JJ that seminars alone are enough to service all obligations. He will then enjoy his profits without any stress.

JJ reminisces at how his friend made tons of money, by supplying campaign material to the present Governor and his team.

Let us now focus on business person number two. KM is another of Apple town's businessmen. He runs a successful hardware store. Two years ago, KM expanded it to include a fabrication workshop.

The school expansion program and the many residents constructing new homes make for a regular and profitable clientele. KM has invested hundreds of millions of shillings in his business.

In nature, KM is a calculating person capable of getting to know, what is happening on both sides of the political divide, without ruffling feathers.

Like many experienced business people, KM follows current affairs without openly exhibiting any excitement.

For many years, KM has made contributions to all sides of the political equation and, it has served him very well because, his customers and walkers-by, see him as one minding his own business.

Back to business person number one. Given the opportunity at hand, JJ argues that one must be the proverbial businessman of all seasons, who finds it prudent, to sell both umbrellas and ice cream at the same time.

When it rains, the umbrellas move and when hot, the ice cream sells fast.

This is the season and with an extra tranche of new project money from the bank, JJ is best placed to deliver the much sort after campaign merchandise. An initial deposit was enough for JJ to get the work done.

KK, an old friend off JJ's, has been patiently waiting the whole day at The Apple hotel, for him to return. KK is the one that initially helped JJ to identify the huge opportunity in the hotel business and, now visits from time to time.

As soon as they meet, KK hits the nail on the head. "JJ, please go easy on politics and focus on your business." "Everyone can see that you are going down badly." JJ shrugs him off as an old, tired and jealous villager with no fresh ideas.

The heightened activity has forced JJ to delegate most hotel duties to his manager. Earlier, JJ had been confidently on top of things and has had all business systems only known in his head.

The manager was the first employee that JJ, hired when he opened the hotel business. This manager had worked in other establishments and, was instrumental in getting many customers through the doors initially.

The manager is known from elsewhere, as the type to easily take advantage of access to the cash coming in from customers.

The insurance broker has come to see the manager on an all-risks insurance policy but, gets turned away. The manager indicates that they are on a cost cutting period.

After helping himself to some of JJ's hotel's money, the manager, three months down the road realizes that 80% of the conference business has gone away to RK's hotel, The New Pluto hotel.

RK has just completed and quietly opened a new outfit. He had researched well enough to know that conference business needs a conducive environment.

RK does not encourage people idling around and his customer service standards are second to none other in town.

Unlike JJ who is now identified with one side of the leadership contest, RK is a neutral observer and has focused his business activities on winning over his core customers.

He is often seen talking to or visiting his big customers, so that he keeps winning their business, over and over again.

Apple town is the main center of activity in Apple County and, like all major towns, gold diggers abound. Successful business people cannot escape the keen eyes of the people preying on their hard earned money.

In Apple town, signs of personal success often trigger nearby predators into action. The promise of euphoric moments is dangled your way in exchange

for a share of your wallet. This side of town is not for the faint-hearted.

JJ is one such person quickly swallowed up by the town's offers. The campaign season, creates a double effect on JJ, sending him into a super ecstatic state that confounds both friends and foes alike.

It no longer matters to him if the money he is using on none-core activities is from the hotel income or withdrawals of the bank loan.

Fast forward, the much awaited day arrives and, every eligible person eagerly exercises his or her democratic right.

A day later, JJ is admitted in a hospital. Results indicate that all his preferred candidates were resoundingly beaten.

They have vanished without settling their huge hotel bills and, the outstanding balance due from supplying the campaign merchandise. A mischievous gang has set on fire the accommodation wing at Apple hotel in celebration.

JJ opens his eyes and now comes to terms with the fact that, he has been in the hospital for two months and, the bank wants to talk to him. He calls for KK and a famous spiritual leader to visit him in the hospital.

That is the end of our case study.

The dashboard below is populated with the risks that we have just gone through. They afflict JJs business.

Rate them on a scale with 1 being extremely bad and 5 being extremely good.

	Risks	1	2	3	4	5
1	Not attracting business					
2	Not retaining business					
3	Political					
4	Lack of cash					
5	Business systems					
6	Reputational					
7	Euphoria					
8	Resources					
9	The arrival pitfall					
10	Latent disdain					
11	Technological					
12	Business environment awareness					
	TOTAL					

Please add up the scores and use the guide overleaf to assess the risk level.

1. 0 to 12 – The business is in critical condition and may not have a high chance of redemption if the situation persists.
2. 13 to 24 – The business is limping badly and requires a lot of effort to attain normalcy.
3. 25 to 36 – the business is on its feet but remains vulnerable to the effects of competition.
4. 37 to 48 – The business is firing on all cylinders and is formidable.
5. 49 to 60 – The business is efficient, admirable, profitable and unshakeable but please do not go to sleep.

What needs to be done to get JJ to 5 on all risks?

Please do the same for your business and work on eliminating or reducing the effects of the risks.

www.ingramcontent.com/pod-product-compliance
Lightning Source LLC
Chambersburg PA
CBHW061202180526
45170CB00002B/927